Yarn

Yarn

Rob Nixon

Copyright ©2020 Rob Nixon
All rights reserved
ISBN-13: 978-1-7327842-7-7
June 2020

Projects Gray

She whispered cruel and proud words,
"I am past it, you are a child, a teenager.
The world is not the way you see it.
Everything has to be taken care of.
It is not hard. We've figured out most things.
You're just going to have to trust us on that.
You are not capable of a deeper understanding."

Plagues

Yesterday, *Ancient Aliens* suggested
viruses may be designed to advance humanity.
The word culling was used.

New List

I hate your dad,
you.

Red Elevator

The dirt is everywhere.
Once the velcroed red carpet is removed,
it goes down with the staff.

Natural Stratum

The aqueduct is completely gone.
The buildings will be gone too.
The people, families, communities,
they are completely lost to history.

A Hit

Those shows with the lost space-time travelers—
being lost is sad.
They should make a show about that, the sadness.
Insulated, fed, oxygenated, in complete absolute nothingness,
a human reduced to that.
Weekly, episodic, no dialog whatsoever,
just for peeping in, checking in.

Feel Guilty?

Not near ready,
not nearly strong enough.
Can't stop them now though,
they're going.

Duel

Sand outposts so far apart,
going there for some reason.
Broiling pavement,
bubbling and chipped paint,
this is an oven.
I am not capable.
I have never been capable.
Life in the sand, on the sand too.
Plants!
Insects, rats, lizards!
It can't be ignored, the heat.
All these things are aware.
I would be sharing this awareness with them,
if I stopped,

and got out—
for about fifteen minutes.
Then shared as protein, flesh, and blood.
On the job fifteen minutes earlier—
my fathers would have been prepared.

Bic Boy

Little gel tip protector,
buckyball,
well almost,
I tossed you carelessly.
I was caressing you. You just happened to be there,
somehow there,
on a piece of paper,
next to a cup of coffee.
At least is what I think you were.
I eat in the bed too.
Hundreds of crumbs,
some rubbed spherical,
what are the odds?
And a zero percent chance of actually finding it.
It'll have to do,
the tan carpet and all,
my eyes,
and it's slightly dirty,
more so underneath.
It is presentable, but,
that will have to be its final destination.
At least until I vacuum.
Stuck in caked fiber maybe?
Maybe until demolition.

Cool.

Admired

Just painful, worn out steps,
that's all.
I'm searching for Yahweh.
Biology is death,
working backward from there,
to here,
a sentient being.
This has to end.

Fold AFB

Two opposite things
existing in the same place,
that is metaphysical nuclear science.
We are experimenting successfully in the desert.

Prime Directives

A lot of fricatives—
that threatening.
Tone is art.

Staged Procedure

I am here and I understand you.
I am the therapist.
Lie down,
prone.
This has to be inserted, don't be alarmed.

I am the office of correction.
That is our relationship.
I am humane.
This has to be supplied.

Enterprise

"Deflector shields up!"
"Photon torpedoes locked on target!"
"Fire!"

Rorschach's

Again? If that's what you want.
Until then,
study the images I have prepared for you.

Usage

Fear and lust are nouns.
Obliged and responsible, qualities.

Honoria

I think you've sussed me out completely.
And almost from the beginning.
I have an almost complete absence concerning you.
What the other guys see, I am not sure.

Baby U

They always found it.
It was analyzed chauvinistically, granted.
Social tolerance of releases—in that too.

The egg is there.

Unrighteous

The strobed and plasmatic energy
has broken diodes and crystals everywhere.
Add to this the fear and distrust,
also add stupidity and violence—
there is no conscience in this thing at all,
stop trying to find it.

Peel

The unmasking is mercifully slow.
It heals as it peels—
tension biometric setting remaining at one.

Idle

I am active.
I am also not burdened with precedent or foresight.
A pack of dogs domesticates the idea
dogs with supplements,
dogs that'll live 'til twenty.

Gi

Greek islands are debris.
Crazy geologic things happen there regularly.
Hearty life there.
Keeps improving.

Outrigger

Being on a commuter ferry
and not being a commuter,
the cold is not endured.

Home

Zoms Zoms caters to them,
every single one of them.
They like being there,
seeing it.
Electric food,
it hums going down.
They are mostly quiet.
They are gold and shiny.

Bad Intuition

Now that talking thing on your neck,
that strobed out, funny thing,
we have to use that these days to get any mates.
It has come to that.
And most of us succeed!
Can that possibly continue?

Give Up

You equate quickness with quiet,
socialism with soviet gray.
And you persist in thinking this way.

Schismatic

A saxophonic nothing score,

a set in someone's memory,
none of it is good—
deleted.
The whole intellect property is changed now.
Wow.

Little Surfer Girl

Oppressed equals dirty.
Dominant, beautiful.
It gets you through the day.
Leaves you unplugged,
mathematics are seen,
reflections of light,
everything.
The personality stumbled into is another story altogether.
That's the board, dude.

Autograft

At nine a.m. on a Saturday morning,
I don't want to be known as being with someone.
It is nobody's business.
That was being selected out of the species,
not anymore.

Cherries

After a few times
you ask yourself,
am I committed to this slot?
Is this a winning chair?
And then there's Franklin from the Twilight Zone.

Franklin

My nickels,
where are my nickels?

Nickels

Sandbags full of them,
tracked up to the banks,
and then back down to the mines to get more—
melted down into new green.

Human Fact

Variations and wavelengths
hit the right chord occasionally,
on the way up,
on the way down.
Stretch these out and arrange them
into something beautiful.

Industrial Morning

Cooked in oil and tar,
washed out with solvent,
it rises up out of the west,
and spreads eastward.

Red Shirt

Scene one, chasing the perp,
seemingly *the* perp,
all kinds of slick getaways,
you would think, scene two, same perp,

but no, T.J. doesn't give up,
no scene two for this guy.

Privacy

Squirrels mating and chattering
with piano practice in the background—
yes, there is a living thing in that tan-yellow box,
that thing behind the tree.

Hook

I am in the car with
someone I just met.
I am the question mark
and the exclamation mark.

No One There

I ring the church.
The past is stubborn.
They call me a madman.
Why do I return?
I want an answer!

Genesis

Drug-induced panic,
desperate cowardice,
neuron storm,
and a new pilot—
the convincer directs things until stability is achieved.
The suggestible masses take this trip too.

They fill in the blanks.

Sessions

High-quality headphones,
brand new equipment,
the most expensive,
master technicians,
here it comes.

Mr. Gray

You heard of Slenderman?
No.
It is an internet legend.
Ok. Never hear from him.
Really clever, dark stranger in chat rooms.
Ok.
Be careful who you chat with.
Lol.
He might say "nice dress" or something like that.
What should he wants from me?
He likes pretty German women.
You're alone, right?
Yeah.
I am a detective.
Ok.
Be careful. I will keep an eye on you.
I am an internet monitor.
I am hardwired into the internet.
I am in your modem.
There is computing going on in here.
10101010101010101010101010

1010101010slenderman1010101010

101010101010101010101010101010

Have you been to the dark web?

No.

Good, if it weren't my job, I wouldn't go there either.

Hot today in Germany?

No.

It's hot in Seattle, omg…

It was raining the whole weekend.

Summer is ending.

Yeah, slowly.

I was created in a Microsoft laboratory.

Ok.

I am lonely.

Ok.

I escape sometimes.

Ok.

Look at my profile.

What is there?

My face.

And?

Full of energy, inside the machine.

Looks more like full of drogs.

I see you.

Ok.

You look very comfortable. Drugs? Lol.

I'm wired, baby.

Buzzbuzzbuzzzzzzzzzzzzzzzzzzzzzzzzzz.

Frankenstein.

I like Germany.

Feels like home.

Slenderman was a kind of ghost-alien-cyborg…

I see.
…who kills or tries to kill mostly kids.
It's really fucked up.
It is just a 21st century ghost story.
Kids really fucking loved it.
Really fucking love it still.
Now there's truth behind the myth.
I was with him for three months,
seven feet tall,
U.S.
I don't remember any of it.
Nothing except in the beginning it was summer
and at the end it was snowing.
I was in the back of an ambulance.
Then back home in Seattle.
Like a spider, fed, I guess.
Nobody missed me at all.
I was just in a coma in a hospital.
People that aren't alive anymore
visited me when I awoke.
Thought there was a loose chip or something.
Hardware guys.
"I have a monkey wrench. I am independently
adjusting your settings. There, all better now?"
I wonder what happened to them?
My mind's a blank.
I have very little organic brain.
I am in your modem.
Sometimes I just have memories.
In one, I have somehow found myself
in a car with a woman after pumpkin picking.
A very beautiful woman.

Rob Nixon

I don't remember anything of what was
talked about on the way to the car or out in the field.
Probably concentrating mostly on not dropping
the damn thing.
Just sitting there is what I remember.
And the muscle and joint pain fading away.
Isolated from the natural air, I could see in the valley
a football field not too far away.
Close enough to see where the band would sit—
the brass in the morning sunshine waiting for them.
And the loud speakers set up for the assembly,
rusty and ready to bring home the point,
I saw the empty bleachers.
The only other thing I remember is that she had five kids.
I am addicted to the telemetry.
I am my own secret project now.
I've learned how to enter the bodies of
really sick people on life support in the hospital,
the ones who are strong,
always men of course,
drug overdoses,
the ones who never get visitors—
I visit them.
I make them better.
And they are discharged!
I really only come to advanced countries,
because, you know, the technology.
There is a 100% transplant rejection rate; the bodies
die pretty quickly.
I try to know when it's time—
get back on life-support.
I am in kitchen making tea.

I know.

Don't Care

I am not going to testify against myself.
I'm the only witness.
I have done nothing wrong.
Since you asked, that is my statement.
Nothing further.

Flank

The ankle to the hip bone,
the lateral side,
that is where you'll find it.
It's vital to understand what the smile means.
And the smile back.
Then the eyes understand.
It's really cool.

Brain Case

The vermilion border is rather abrupt.
That is where the skin begins.
The face is the first thing.
Then the rest of it.

Abyss

There is no depth there.
Worn away by the magma.
It is crust.
It really does swallow people up.

It is dangerous.

She Is Gone

Oh, I am awake and alive,
but in darkness, in a drain.
This sense of smell thing is whack, geez!
And it's too warm.
I must be pretty far down, the absolute furthest,
no miracle here.

Drips

I stay on the molar side that doesn't give way.
I see everybody flowing out.
Gravity plummets them.
I draw nearer to the margins.
I believe in the flow now,
I am not antagonistic to it anymore.
It is there to assist the individual.
It is there to help them reach their full potential.
Everyone is better off.

Advancement

Why are their smiles so different?
Their anger so strange?
Their leaving keeps me up.
That is the gradient.
Up close, you're so different.
I paint it.
And it is beautiful.
That thought draws me dangerous.

The Deal

Get the most mentally deficient member
of the other group to speak.
If that person is a bully, they will have support.
The negotiation and points trend toward yourself then.
This is kung fu.

Locus

It is a piece of art made of wood.
It will not be thrown away, it will be kept.
Even by those who find it among the remains.
What did it look like new?
What sort of person recognized it?
How many years unseen?

Reps

Musty, loud, gripping hands,
swing, turn, flip,
miss and fall into the net again.
Climb back on,
turn the same twist.

Assembly

Everyone's talking with one another,
almost everyone. And they're fully active.
Even the alone ones are caught up in it.
They float above it too.
And there they are noticed on the radar.

Paying

I will help you manage your life.
You will think of things correctly from now on.
Drinks in glasses, lipstick,
things left on the floor—
and in the morning, there is no love again.

Spectral Choir

There is a raise now in the labyrinth,
from the outside, through the tubes.
A thousand little tendrils are
each picking up the same spasm, tremor.
It is uninterrupted.
It is a crowd without the physical vibration.

Immune System

Set up something supernatural
to hone an intelligence
already supernatural,
and we scramble up out of it.
Cells know how to destroy one another.
And now we do too.
This insider knowledge presses
an already infinite advantage.
We squeeze matter and anti-matter at once.

Museum of Flight

I have been selected,
I am being led down a long hallway,
not part of the museum itself,

to a room that is all white.
There is an enormous light-blue painting hanging there,
twenty-five feet tall, fifty feet long.
It is three cubes stacked on three cubes,
alternating light on dark ice blue,
blurred margins—
meant to be viewed far away.
It could be a flag; viewed on both sides,
the image would be almost identical.
One of the squares looks scuffed,
or burned by a buffer—
lower left, wind blowing east,
lower right, wind blowing west.

TV

They mature out there,
await their canceled future.
The viewers are waiting to press themselves into them.
It is always the answer,
the perfect response.

Aetolian Soil

The doctors wanted the prisoners' bodies.
Open them up.
Then came the poets.
They noted the paralyzed cries.
They examined the fibrous cords,
where they connected, where everything.

Diseased Monkey

More organically pure,
a contagion source,
it knows something's up,
all the hazmat suits.

Quitclaim

Slid in fast between two clauses
was the article concerning perception.
It was sixty words of saying the ends justify the means.
A few rows down was the expectation. The fullest weight
of the law was mentioned.
And down near the end was a declaration of equality.

Woods

The ones that lap up the water
are from the less advanced tribes
or all alone.
Their sojourn less planned, their organization
probably just brutal.

911

Stop calling the police.
They aren't going to do anything about it.

Seed

Something else is happening.
It will supplant this reality.
Another kind of meaninglessness.
This will happen tomorrow.

Economic Growth

What are the things to remember?
I am comfy,
my room has no fists,
and meaninglessness will prevail.
Trust in that.

Art Gallery

I am going to be 1910.
We are a movement,
we are the collective,
we are a cult.

Sedimentation Rate

Swaying and delirious,
I am left to wander the city
alone.
The debris of society, I pass by.
I immerse myself in them.
So many colors looking so gray.
Black and white doesn't capture this.

Blood Stain

The night's muscle—
the cats stay away, the rats.
The shadow remains still.
It is usually a hard thing, lots of pain.
The fear is totally justified.

Chimp's Grin

The ones in the nature footage
are much more interesting.
They don't know the world they live in.

Iconoclasts

Some survive in the blood as memory B cells.
Mass psychosis is a two-way street.

Pirate Radio

A name flashes by and a memory,
words heard,
secondhand music,
and that people are reacting.

Surrender

You've fallen into a solid offensive strategy.
Liquor cabinet whiskey,
next door roses—
do not look this situation in the eye.

Story Arc

You did,
I was created,
something is out there.
I do,
it will happen to you,
no more other.

Beer Glasses

Breathe in the noise at intervals,
break up the rhythm.
Think of uptown sunshine
and gray days out of town.

Help

I am getting it.
Suspicions of it are not dismissed anymore.
It has become a fact.
A catalyst brings it to the surface,
makes it a reality.
Not again.

Impressions

What is happening in the darkness?
Are my friends being wounded?
(This is still planet Earth.)
Most of it is positive.
Things are going as planned.
(I am still a hominid.)

Naughty

It's some kind of overt thing,
not subtle.
It will be directly to me.
This would have caused a psychotic response in the past.
The reaction is the goal.

Changed

The shame of it cancels it out,
but you do feel pleasure.
The two things together produce the shell,
one coating against the other.
I am jealous.

Wandering

Impulse control,
no sleep,
anxiety disorder,
substance use—
victim.

Don't Aside

It just produces anxiety in real.
Driving alone and cursing at bad drivers, really?
It does not achieve a dramatic effect.
As a comedic device it works fine.

Friend

Movement con acento,
that is the person to look for,
the one apart,
that person is the member of the species,
there are photos,
there is a laughing.
there is food.

Watch

Nick Chopper's parents died—in Oz.
No one dies in Oz.
They can be killed, they live forever otherwise.
Munchkins can be different.
Nick Chopper was different.
That guy didn't understand.

Mono

All the words were said,
the beats heard,
I guess I was internalizing before,
and they were blended into a single, finite unit.
Hearing them more separate now.

Expression

Philosophy is harnessing the heart.
Then one thing leads to another
and in a few hundred years you're on the moon.
There are no great moon adventures, no moon men.

In a Back Room

Urban warfare could be going on out on the streets right now,
intense neighborhood battles,
heroism being manifested every few minutes,
ammunition runs, strategy, leadership,
bravery shot in the face,
what I was dropped on this Earth for,
and I wouldn't be there.

Bystander

I am the first to see it,
and get all the attention.
The praise feels good.

Mass

Prick it free from its adhesions.
Scrunch down low.
Scoop, scrape, brush.
Normal saline flush.
Scoop, scrape, brush.
Normal saline flush.
A stump of the thing itself now,
but still…

Dirty

They were not picky about the nutrients they were given.
Against gravity and polluted, the gray beards survived.

Sweaty

The immune response tastes tangy.
It tastes warm too.

The Nerve

I will not be laughed at.
But I have done it, and hard too.
God!
So? That is buried.
I don't think about that much.

I blurt out words.
I shake my head.
No!

Astronauts

A rocket taking off through the atmosphere—
a communion unexplainable.
In a psychological sense,
use and abuse are both disease terms,
trending downward.

Subterranean

Everything has completely gone wrong.
Everything is perfect.
Usually nearer the first.
That's not the anxiety.
It's those two possibilities, plural, against reality.
Fictions and fact create this anxiety.
It pivots and burrows from the possibilities.
It is mobile underground.
It becomes a three-way activity.

Trillion Trillions

The ecosystem is in very delicate balance.
Nature is stable.
The bugs can gather here.
Alteration is permanent.
Substitute *psychosystem*.

Foreign

The 100% I think about is not even 1.
I used to even imagine the supernatural.
The 99% has to be carried around with you
(this conversation were having now never happened),
but something seems wrong,
there is a little bit of the incorrect in it.

Trespass

Can you influence yourself?
I do believe it affects the body,
but not down to the cellular level.
That doesn't happen.

Thud

We are all just like the Egyptian
face half-down in the soil,
smiling about all the bad things
that have been going on lately,
that's now led to this,
dying probably.
All the splashes are the workers.
They are still going about it.
It doesn't even matter.
The grain glistens.

Mummy

Under the paw they kept digging,
extending its arms.
It's really protected down there.
The bones are still knit together.

Skin still intact.
They must not have thought much about
the aesthetic beauty of the cat,
just its function.

Giza Plateau

It is the playpen
of the child
who was busy all day
babbling
and laughing,
building and blocking.

Jack

Hacked up out of the ground,
scooped out clean,
fresh candle in the hollow.

Interview

"What look were you going for?
A cheap man in a cheap suit?"
That begins the first half of it…

Lowest Percentile

My report will be filed as soon as I get back to my office—
go see a therapist!
My goodness, it's probably too late now!
It will be too late in thirty minutes anyway.
Look at you! Look at your housing unit!

See all this blue, here? Hello? You there?
On the walls? That's usually a sign of something bad.
Wow!
I would get a lung x-ray.
Never mind, they will give you one, free of charge.
You people are never clean.
With Austerity, I can't believe they even bother.
This form is all blue too.
It's all about you—blue pen.
Like I said, I can't believe they even bother.

Mom

She was right about that,
they did hate her.
But the part about the plots against her,
she was wrong about that.
Nobody wanted to have anything to do with her.
That part is hard to accept.
The plots and things are way more appealing.
If you stay smart and observant, reality never goes away,
no matter how appealing the other shit is.

Home Baked Cookies

The norms know they are abused. It is their burden.
I'm sure the reality of being attacked never goes away.
The goody-goody stuff must be appealing.

And It's the Future!

That's the reward for us both.
It is co-occurring disorder along with

all the other delusions.
Unrelated I think; we are hominids,
we think about things like that.

Suppressed

I change my dressings twice a day now.
I am in constant need of wound protection.
Open sore, immunocompromised—
it will get better.

Years

Who knows how fast we're moving?
In every sense of the word, we occupy different space.
There is zero and one.
Inside the zero are physical laws.

The Account

There was some kind of gun thing going on,
smuggling.
Businessmen are used who have been compromised.
Everything is there before them.
The organization, the labor—
and that's all it is.
There's no clandestine meetings,
no hand wringing.
And it's the patriotic thing to do.

Pedigree

Wanting to say the right thing

at the right time
with the correct tone.
Making people feel good,
and rage at times.
He was just about there,
my father.

Transaction

What is the principal?
It has to do with ownership.
The money has been lent, it is gone,
free to use by the recipient.
Certain oaths are made on a benefit in return.
The business is interest.
Curious people.

Scapegoat

Some people ritually kill,
slash the throat,
victims,
sacrificial animals.
It is if I, the target, am to say,
"I live, I must repay."
No.
I can accept this energy.
I can accept it as a gift.

Oath

The oath is missing.
The oath is usually taken by force,

and violently,
mind and body,
mostly mind,
or what they think is mind.
An Rx is needed sometimes.
But I am resistant,
I overflow,
the negative is positive,
I overwhelm and take.

Mistaken Identity

That is the sick and twisted thing.
And it is retained knowledge too!
Why I do things is always wrong!

Groan

Ideals are simple
and hard to define.
Easier to contrast,
that's where the bigotry comes in.
These are very difficult times.

Tacky

The *I am not that* doesn't apply anymore.
That is not an acceptable answer.
The offenders are forced to just leave,
no longer participate in anything.

Trapped

What are the recall indicators?
Through the roof.

Cob

Hatched out a week early
in the warm environment.
(At some point, he just really liked everything about music.
Liked the people, liked the fans.
He was a punk rocker.
He wanted it to sound good.
And the words.
That's what it was about.)
Soft remnant, red husks in the background,
he ate every single one of them.
Hatched out protein in the end.
Then crawled out magnificent.

Truth Serum

There will always be a man.
It will always be the same man.
One hundred percent confident—
everything about the self and the world around,
jazzed.
Not only is what he's saying the absolute truth,
he's doing it with style,
he is beautiful.

Free Expression

You mean there are actual people
who can't accept a viewpoint opposite from theirs

so much so
that any expression of it
cannot go unanswered?
Loudly and in mobs?
"This hominid's mouth is shut!"
There are people like that?
Seattle is absolutely full of them.

Las Vegas

Piled up five miles high everywhere,
surviving just barely at every single layer,
slowly evaporating away—
so much in space and orbit,
rings around the Earth.
It is a wonder,
different wavelengths,
different eyes,
I see them as angels.

Post

It is army men.
Just gathering them all up,
positioning them with power—
this is how they're all fed,
this is how brained.

Options

I don't think it's me I'm protecting.
It's the ones who organize, man,
the one's who want to run things—

travel will be regulated.

Plant-Based Plastics

I want to go to the flower shops in my neighborhood.
They're everywhere here.
But they're not the same.
I want those here.
I want them here and all alone on a weekday,
cloudy and bright.

Decimation

A trigger for each finger squeezed into a fist,
not aimed, just mad,
eyes closed tight.

Heavy Blocks

I have no direct connection with current events,
but I am what is happening.
This is confirmed
when I listen to the music
and to the words,
listen to what's there—
but there is no *real* there.
One delusional guy wearing headphones all by himself.
No TM, no dream walking, no other personality,
none of that.
I've convinced exactly one person.

RIP

After that, you just go around
and make flowers grow.
When I am not here, man, nothing's here.
Just natural cycles going on endlessly.

Corrective Action

I am not instigating anything.
There is no outcome I work toward.
I am in the flow.
Those other two things
produce the ridiculousness we're involved in here.

Future Endeavored

There is the possibility of layoffs now.
That thought has dropped in the bucket.
And I believe it to be true.
And its opposite, that is true too.

Marginalized

All the best efforts up in smoke,
not prevented even with extraordinary efforts.
It is the same thing, I go by the percentages too,
I can hardly criticize them for doing that.

Fated?

That would have to be helped along the way,
the extremest chance of probability
on multiple occasions,
and after the fact reassurances.

The facts are shining there in my memory all alone.
Absolutely no one would believe any of them.

Heads

Any kind of success data
that this thing could produce is cooked.
There is something going on ancillary, up a sleeve,
makes it appear that this has any kind of positive effect.
It is probably some kind of middle management bloodbath
that raises things.
This gives the image of a lean workforce.
It also lowers salaries.
The stuff down to the classified staff
just seems pulled out of someone's ass.

Macro

Expecting a coming together
like children,
cooperating and playing nice,
forming *together* meetings,
training ourselves—
this instead of someone
who knows exactly what to do
showing someone who doesn't know what to do
what to do—
just seems stupid.
I'm sure in your business and management classes,
you were given examples of bad management,
bad departments—
things can be done badly.

Sex Scene

People do use this site for recreational purposes.
I don't know if you have a blog, a diary, or just a bestie,
but you will have stories to tell.
Every time you think of it, it will be,
"I met men on that site."

Strangers

The car door shutting doesn't work for me anymore.
The brightly lit interior,
the muffled voices,
the sounds,
the expensive motor,
the traffic, the turns,
the lights,
the romantic music, low music,
the scene makes me very uncomfortable.

Adjudicated

The trogs that advance out
will be appropriately segregated; our psychology
department is huge.

The Can't Touch

What does the extreme negativism,
the vulgar abuse,
accomplish?
The touch but don't touch,
the guilt, the fear,
these pre-exist your outburst,

these pre-exist in me.
Your abuse is the skeleton key.
You may receive a shotgun blast to the face on entry.

Further Action Required?

When you've turned the other cheek, you've given wisdom and advice. You're discharged.

Natural

It will always be artificial
until you go out and create the sub-species.
That would require absolute authoritarianism
for at least twenty years,
North Korean style authoritarianism.
The medical wing will have to remain on lock down
for at least that long. Control will have to remain absolute there,
even if more freedom is phased in elsewhere.
Twenty-year blocks of correction and perfection
will be carried out in thousands of cities worldwide.
Experts have gone over the data.
They suggest sixty years, three blocks, short time frame.
And one hundred twenty years, long time frame.
How many subspecies cannot reasonably be imagined.
Six seems to be the starting block.
It may remain that way,
increase, or decrease.
None of the subspecies will be allowed for space travel.

Creeping

I'd rather not be clearly identifiable.
It makes you pay attention to what I'm saying.
The cat meowed.

2020

Door wide open and exit sign,
staff restroom right next door,
flushing and going home.
I think I am the last appointment; I've been sitting
here long enough.
I want to see if they're looking as they pass me by,
they are not supposed to stare.
(He looked at my eyes and said they're good.
Then he talked about healthcare.)

Polite Society

You will always get a more brutal response.
A *"should this person be killed?*
will always get an *of course!*
Along with a long list of others—
has not hundreds of years of civilization
been taught in the schools?

Front Yard

I do not go ask for help!
I am a dog barking on a chain.
I like watching and listening.
I like talking!

Change Agent

It's not actually bad to be a poor clinical outcome.
The medical professionals at the institution
where things like this are read and understood,
the judges of outcomes
after all the data has been shaken out,
they want to see poor outcomes.
It is a number for change, improvement.

Guess Jeans

It is the people tired of being themselves,
the blue neon in the darkened room,
the loud music,
the alcohol,
and the shiny colors.

Famous

The investigation concluded he was a true split personality.
There was a strong dissent. "No pure evidence at all
except the photograph
which could have been totally innocent."
The dissent mostly focused on a willingness to believe
one single person was the subject of many pop songs.
A man that can be woman sometimes,
a shape-shifting karma chameleon,
one actual person,
invading people's minds at night,
implanting realities,
informing the narrative a million miles away.

Famous, Baby

Sexually speaking, "baby" had changed completely
since the seventies. It is spirit now.
This is understood by artists.
And understanding it does not destroy it!
Their art is simply a discussion of this reality.
It is being sung consciously.
The report writers were convinced of this.

Art Not

Singing is a youthful activity.
And expressing it as "baby" is natural—
seventies before and after.
Instead they believed the guru thing.

Art History

It began as a small lie.
It was meant to delay a kidnapping.
A lie that he might have money,
he may have written songs.
It was spun officially somewhere in Washington.
More fictions were added to it.
Each meticulously grafted upon the ones that came before.
"Why doesn't he go out?" An answer comes from Langley.
All these militia types
scratching their heads about this grunge character
as information came in.
And it all ends up with him being in this split personality state.
That's it.
A fictional bio written by some nameless bureaucrat,
and made into some sort of reality by the two agents in charge.

Art Too

"What did you say to that Nazi?"
"Haha! How did you know?
No, a cop or something gave me $500
to say I knew some guy in a photo,
that I was worried about him.
They wanted me to press up close to the guy
and ask him if he knew where the kid was.
They wanted me to, you know,
be obnoxious and aggressively curious.
I think they think it ends these things quicker.
Less chance the barfly makes a mistake—who knows?
I think I was believable. He did leave pretty quickly."
"I saw that guy at the spa. He is a Nazi.
I'm glad he's gone."
"He'll soon be in prison.
I don't think the other Nazis in there
will put up with him either.
Remember him the way I do, young and virile"
"And gone."
"He might look back on this day.
Remember how sunny and warm…"
"And humid,"
"…rainbow colors everywhere,
how happy everyone seemed,
how good you looked sitting there…"
"Ha!"
"…probably on his third to last night,
knowing it's one of his last nights,
knowing they've found out about him.
He'll probably wonder what it feels like
to have your balls cut off.

Or hang yourself.
He will wonder about that day,
today,
that he should have stopped the case,
should have stopped being a detective,
should have created a new identity,
gotten a cash job,
just been a working slob,
maybe meeting a hot chick and settling down,
not being himself anymore—
remember him young and virile."
"And gone."

Lost Art

Youth is also sad when it is gone.
Hence, sad songs.
It is a natural connection
every day for the last ten thousand years.
It is a noticeable pattern when pointed out.
That and the happy youth, baby.

Artist

At some point he was aware of it.
His heavy drug use,
his isolation except for controlled personnel—
he was absolutely surrounded by a truth
that everyone except he was aware of.
But he became aware of it.
First there was the fear, *there was death*.
This fact absolutely surrounded him.
Not his death though,

not his own delayed torture and murder,
but his friend's!
How did the story go?
He imagined a love affair with his friend's wife!
And she secretly loved him!
This dawned on him.
The Washington D.C. stuff came later.
I guess it's the company you keep.
He was soaking it all in.
The fusion happened with love.
The murder and everything else came next.
He became aware.

Creator Art

The nail and hammer are on one side.
The board on the other.
He became the hammer
before their eyes.

(Hysteria)

A paranoid schizophrenic
out of control,
talking to the police,
not safe to be around,
a mad man.

Death of Art

A termination,
everybody frozen,
all business shot,

investigation pointless.

Pop Art

This small little drama,
with its white nationalist, sado-masochistic undertones,
must have had legs.
It has lasted to the present day.
It is remembered every day by those involved.
The functional paranoid schizophrenic,
or fake one,
or recovered one,
seemed the only one oblivious to it.
Frozen by choice?
He just went back to a humming solitude,
a patterned, predictable life,
a focused looking forward,
everything the same,
rotated clothes, recipes,
the music inside him,
grinding his teeth away.

Artist Critic

No court cases, no prison, no hospital,
just line up at the marijuana store,
show your I.D.,
get in the queue,
get your prescription filled,
and go back to your room.
Consider that.
I would want to see my records.
That is how it would begin.

There would be words in it
like sexual deviant,
thief,
liar,
and coward.
Instead of me looking up at myself for my separation,
it would be me looking at the facts.
In reality, my behavior would be the result of a treatment plan.
Everything would be the complete opposite of what I thought.
Seeing patterns in things without one
is diagnosed with paranoid schizophrenia.
I would read that.

I Accept That

Paranoid delusions are always factually wrong.
I accept that too.
These two things are in my thinking all the time.
Not just wrong thinking though; remember,
complete opposite.
Being targeted for removal from society.
Not me seeing all culture as being detrimental to the human.
No, this culture sees this human as detrimental.
And gives good Rx to the patient,
enforces the protocol—
more thoughts, more inactivity,
more peering through the blinds.
This is much more efficient than institutionalization.
And it more than pays for itself.
It's just medication management.
Arranging it, the cloak and dagger stuff,
is probably easy to manage too.

We just line up for it.
My behavior is not good, it's bad.
And it's not mine, it's public.
It would have to follow that my art would be the same.
What is the opposite of poetry?
The opposite of painting?
Cliched commonplaces?

Life as Art

A separation, another probable walking the streets—
a hammer and a nail.

Art Repository

All the real documents will be beyond suspicion.
They will be appropriately dated and on the right paper.
The classified factual ones, the myths, and the present mess
are all somewhere.

Future of Art

The unexplained cognizance from before
is now rivaled by
the power of suggestion he is now unleashing.
The exact same thing is now being manifest in 2020
as in 1992.
He understood it and, now,
at the perfect time,
he is utilizing it.

Chronic Artist

The voices have to speak about today, right?
And about this dimension?
When that's doubted, I will tell the future
or astral plane,
so help me.
Slap that left once in a while.
You have to be punished.

Report

Scope shot, one floor above
and a hundred feet away—
the window is open!
The screen is hardly disturbed.
Traffic, imitating the wind,
streams in louder through the hole,
blood and brains everywhere.

Meats

I must have done so.
In the beginning, I must have.
People mentioning the other times,
the lucid and then lost times,
those experiences,
the absolute pleasures,
the being undetected,
the story continuing
over and over,
the jazzy and poetic times.

Clearer

Having a double life that continues unabated,
a life that completely satisfies every sensuous desire
repeatedly,
and on the other,
a terrified, perfected individual.

1994

If you can suppress pain with a smile,
it follows that other tricks are possible.
Raising your hand when you're not sure,
wouldn't that activate intelligence?
What stops this before it begins?
Losing and the fear of losing are not small things.
We're not in a pristine environment either.
People exploit this adventurousness all the time.
They will take the place of your inner censor gladly.

Wonder

They think I've gone crazy.
Some kind of malignancy or something.
But that it's created some beauty.
A good is being created,
but that there is a pathological reason for it.
Can't there be an original neural experience?
Pathology usually turns things off.
I am turned on.
(They think my editor has been turned off.)

Explain Things

He doesn't want much.

Feels guilty when he does.
Lucidly recognizing someone from that other life,
accidentally,
in public—
he talks in that instance,
not to impress but to cover,
to drown,
to squelch.

This Feels Good

The sooner the better.
My numbers are variable.
Enough to release me?
I guess where I am,
the concept of being released is desirable.
The motions must be passed by a majority,
I do know that much,
two out of three must agree.

Low Information

The man threw the stick
but he still has it behind him.
It is beyond me.
This has taken all the fun out of fetch.

Quiz

Maddy asked me to style the WAM project this year.
And before I've known it, I've agreed to it.
I don't know what the WAM project is.
I've wasted an hour, now, trying to figure that out.

My whole schedule is ruined.
And knowing this company, it could be a trick.
I've utterly failed.
Every second this continues my psyche is damaged.

Ministry

I am conscious and I should not be.
There will be attendants soon.
There are weapons in here.

Selfishness

Just thinking about too many egos—
wouldn't that be something I would want?
Busted, I am a hypocrite.

Grace

It is the devil running like mad,
catching all the manna as it drops.
The manna is three-dimensional.

Everything and Nothing

I believe they know everything about me.
They should know nothing about me.
Lovers, jobs, government stuff—
I imagine Willie (idiot) and Steve (nice guy),
I image Imogene (thief), the other Steve (regular Joe).

All Any of Us Can Do

I am only touching the outside of things,

things that might be true, what people might believe.
It just backs up preconceived ideas,
puts it in a new way.

Could Have Been

I look him in the glasses.
I am someone else! I am!
I do not break the law.
I do not break the law.

Biblical

There was a line in *JFK* that said the bottom line was that
the plotters have to win.
Everything comes down when you lose.
Everything!

Focused

One glass will spin microscopically—
fingertips, don't spill, listen.

Circling

I most certainly do not want to land.
I see it down there,
the crushed bodies,
the impact,
all that.
It is inevitable but I'd just assume continue going around.

Boardroom

A hand pounded on the table,
a succession is taking place—
real life examples, real world success,
a résumé,
a communication to everyone in the entire world.
Pinned up against sacred institutions,
young and unknown versus established,
statement made and scattering.

Berry

Sometimes I can almost imagine it,
walking with rhythm,
driving with rhythm,
having places to go,
a schedule,
projects,
art.

Social

That person has a right to exist too.
The one who wants murder all the time,
who wants jails,
punishment, blood,
teeth, body parts—
that person who exists in their cowardly non-violence,
that person too.

Loins

I seem to remember just a blunt happiness,
a giddiness.

Physically, I felt it in the thighs,
then in the hands.
Spread possibly trying to rub the thighs out.
I think there was an immune response in that.
There was sweating and an awkward hanging down there.

Portrait of the Politburo

Beg off attending the kaffeeklatsches,
become unreliable,
isolate your way away from it,
change your name.

Act I

They are always trying to get me
on some kind of security violation,
revealing official secrets.
But since I am not cleared to know,
I can't know, and thus don't know.

Murder

Getting a hot dog in the park—
hmm, I wonder what that means?
I stare.
It must have kicked ass looking like you.
I'm an old man in a park, alone—
too long.
1:15 at the abandoned boat launch,
a hot dog today, December 1st.
I will buy myself one every day.
A routine becomes invisible.

Learn what she does
and when.
Just like that.
Windbreaker, blue and green,
Wednesday, December 1st,
raining.
The lake looks bigger, farther across,
staring—
I've have stayed too long! I am viewed!
Frozen breath,
frozen breath,
good-bye.

Vacation

When you land and get there,
it's always disappointing.
Then fourth gear sets in
and good times are manufactured.

Score

Giving, bribery, tribute—
the people right in front of you are not the problem,
the things they give you are not bad either.
That does not mean you join with them.

Electroman

Stimulate the CSF,
activate the glandular matrix.

Scientist Sex

A perfected human
on top of a perfected human.

Basic Rule

Everyone ignores some causes,
never give them a second thought.
You can't possibly be offended by that.

Canopy

The hardly eating orangutan
slips to another branch.
Going to lie down and study from there.
Flies land on his hand, crawl around a bit,
then fly away.
A snake slides down the same tree.
The forest bed is noisy.
One of the clacks in the arbor was a mouse,
the rest were more falling leaves.
"This is a warm breeze."

Auto

Okay, here is the logic of the machine,
get your product distributed as soon as fucking possible,
come back, get some more, keep doing this.

Robbie Explains It All

The rhythms that aren't statistical
are still together somehow.
Fit words in there to fill that.

Do that over and over again.
These are not conjured.
There is no spirit behind them at all.
They are just humming out loud turned into singing.
They are just doing that.
They haven't anything better to do.
Any truth that is in there is commended
for its representation of a very small truth
in context.
We also like it when it digs into people we disagree with.

Beauty

The championship team in commune farming
is probably a goddamn impressive thing.
And a positive thing is being done.

Drink Responsibly

Success in business does not validate the business.
Selling poetry does not sanctify it.
A distillery is a good example.
It has something to do with the way words sound.
And people being ready to hear it.

Perceptions

When you detect more movement in the suburbs,
you are right, people actually have lives there.
That is a good thing.
When you feel more touched downtown,
I am not sure.

Idealism

Massive amounts of drugs
have to supplement this emptiness.
Below all the esoteric, there you will find it,
even there on the dirty floor.

Methodical

Everybody might howl about the end product,
continuing in the manic state is the real goal.

Cowboy

Stop by the checkout stand.
Maybe buy a book on Shelley.
Here is a place to be.
Try to avoid subjects.
Do this forever.

Obsessions

There is a lot of supernatural that is swallowed.
It doesn't meet with much critical scrutiny.
It just takes up residence
in safe houses
running games.

Schism

It did feel so foreign
wearing comfy wool socks next to the fire
in the chalet.
Driving up to the mountains and sharing stories,

I hated everything about that.

Location

Where it happened, that is half of everything.
School, how ironic.
In dreams,
we are reminded.
Often, we are falling.
Not just undressed and unprepared,
alone.

Blood Face

I tattooed a butterfly on the inside of my ear,
call me Daisy.
I wear tight, tan pants that show my thighs,
I am a lion.
This is full skeletal.

First One

How was he doing it? Probably walking,
not scurrying around like something real.
But he did look at me.
There were others.
Some of those were scurrying.
The first one merely walked.
I bet he could run fast.
These woods are nice.

Boots

It's not the two inches from your face,
bad breath smelling,
is-this-perfectly-clear,
but it's just as relentless.

Pointlessness

There is no symbolism
in a spider building a web and sitting there
in the middle of my house.

Diamond

Then Jared chipped in his two cents,
and altogether we came up with a nickel.
Luckily, that is what the soda pop cost.
Hot sand, ball field, no one else there.

It Is a Proof

It has to flow out,
be on the loose.
Don't curse the escaped.
Lost forever—seriously, forever.
A good groove gone elsewhere.

FOIA

Contact *Chickadee*,
distribution 103% (1.69 kg.),
personnel 125% (2),
attendance 101% (159),
user intervention *GN* "…unstable and antisocial",

armed, self-harm 89%, assault 33%.
Contract prepared for 6 new personnel.
Increase in ceiling, 3 months, £25,000.
Six units, six years—sorry about yesterday. Sometimes it
feels we are the outsiders. He is going to die. I have
prepared them. There will be papers,
make sure they are distributed.

Windy

Orange and red, it is fall.
They've found a tree and are eating.

Capital

Every dollar spent loses more.
The dollar has a negative effect.
Reasoning does the same thing.

Modem

The lion swallows the museum.
It doesn't do it any good.
It isn't nourished.
It is stopped.

Can't Help It

Small rope,
duct tape,
metal bar…

Business Opportunity

$50,000 to keep quiet.

Control

It won't be too long 'til someone like you
comes in and says that there is no longer a choice,
that I *am* going to the next meeting.

The Realm

Making it a fact is shamanistic.
Making it a perception in others is astral projection.

Pressed

He is following closely behind me,
turns, stops, all that.

Dash

I want the visible spectrum all at once.
If that offends anyone, that is your problem.
I will stay by myself, but still,
it is definitely your problem.

Love Buzz

I think of it like a battery.
You can handle your behavior.
You will know exactly what to do.
I'll just open up the back every once in a while.

Above

Positive space becomes sentient,
and I witchcraft the outside.

Scat

What is the latest babble of reality?
I simply must know.

Visitors Center

I will immerse myself in the resting, layover area.
I will sit down next to myself and listen to my own story,
my rehearsed truth.

UAM

The computer creates art.
Lately, it's literature all has to do with infection.
The database of the immune system is being removed.
Good works will be coming again.

Disease Progression

The disease in the neural matrix,
like an antibody,
has fit in bond by bond
with the false reality that used to be there.

Exposed and Beautiful

I return to my covalent bonds of amnesia.
All the realities are there,
too many,
they confuse.

Add It to the List

Could I pick a different thing to be evil?
To be the thing to be stomped out?
Or is that another thing?

Human Form

The human shape is pasted. It is ugly and awkward.
What caused the documented manic episode?
The opposite of hate and death is love.
The little man in pink is sad looking.
Sharp, sudden sounds cannot be overcome.

Guarded

I have found myself in the general population.
This is critical—
this place does not treat undiagnosed mental disorders!
I am "observed", a diagnosis is "pending".

Afflicted

One person—
one beautiful, loving, tattooed person is in the corner.
I must approach.
Wait—there are more.

Possible Realities

Even though the neural pathways operate in reality,
alternate ones operate too.
Carbon copies made of nitrogen or something.
Different, but account for the same facts.

There has to be another word for believe!

Influence

The building blocks of scenarios
are on top of one another.
It has the devil of reality perfecting it,
troubleshooting it in real time.
It has all the ingredients of art.
It becomes a loud, violent expression, at times.

Self-Analysis

Block out for demographics—ding!
If I think of myself that way,
the category of me,
many kinds of scenarios can be built,
piece by piece with smiles and accidents.

Noob

It is challenging enough for me to navigate reality.
What usually is and what usually happens
is totally trusted. Do I fade away?
No! It's strange, I should.

Shell

There is also a strong belief in the overarching things.
The ones that have left definition,
and only exist in the smiles and accidents.

Bacteria Will Grow

The culture is slapped down,
and the blocks are placed,
building higher and higher.
This culture is inorganic.
It does not metabolize, grow, or synthesize.
It is not a dynamic substance.
When it's slapped on farther up,
it does not change, in-seam, lower down.

Architects

The pyramid builders persuaded
tens of thousands of people
to stop pointlessly speculating on things.

Edge

Marching out of lost
and into rest,
it is just around the corner.
There I won't settle,
my movement will continue.

Aggressor

If anything, you're in a sort of ping.
I add a virus or two.
I am an engineer.

Below You

When you lose the pain,
when you're above,

you lose the opportunity
for continuing life.

Indigo to Red

Crossing paths, discussions, challenges,
sandals, hair, perspiration—
I won't call you or contact you in any way.

Nerve at Night

Peripherally comfortable with a light show above,
no one is looking,
I will slip away and talk with you.

New Reality

They're going to look at you,
then look at me,
and they're going to say,
"Seriously, what the fuck?"

Thousands

Respond appropriately?
What am I worried about?
I know how to do that.

Fitting Room

Changing hues to avoid detection,
subtle coloration, variation on a theme,
anything.

Maybe

I have been totally clueless in the past.
What says that's not now? Another instance.
I have a fixation that I'm seeing
not quite what's really happening.
But I remain confident in my perceptions.
I flux in between them.

My Will

Everybody that gets it
dies right after.
No time to write about it,
post about it,
raise awareness,
nothing.

Combat

The hardcore and impossible to convert
are not even talked about.
Whatever woods they exist in are foreign to me.
Everybody else exists in the reasonable.
And reasonable usually takes the easier choice.
Many adjectives instead of easier,
more than half of them have the word "not" before them.

Censorship

Has anyone ever mentioned
about the plastic-ness of the masks
and not their ugliness in episode 42?

Plastic

Having that quality is not a good thing.
Granted, it is better than zealotry.
Other than that…
Every single hominid immediately recognizes it.
You exist and prosper at their sufferance.
Your money and talent can influence at that time only.
Lose that,
and the money and talent have the opposite effect.

Cries and Panic

It is curative, this revelation.
And composed for that purpose.
There is glee in your ruin.
And ego in the diagnosis.

Acts

Logic recognizes anomalies,
but it acquiesces when it is vetoed.
It totally buys into the metrics.
Logic sees anger and sadness out of place.
This overreach has yet to be resolved.
It deserves the full attention of the committee.

Stonehenge

How bad must this place have been.
And how bad other places just like it.
Most of them have been forgotten.

The Exactlies

We find homes for each other.
Don't go do too many things.
Just can't deal with it.
This used to be kind of celebrated, non-conformity,
now it's an illness.

Snake Dance

The chiefs do not do a head count.
That is really a mystery; that should be a top priority—
all that work polishing the metal, painting the masks,
this will ensure fertility, the harvest!
But no, they don't want to know about the ones
who think the whole thing is just stupid.

Awe

It evenly spills out and covers with repetition,
becomes worthy.
A rare note unintentional is then noticed—
homo sapiens awakes and is at war with Earth.

Right

No docks, no lakes, parks, parties,
I feel I am trespassing.
Just pick up the supplies, pay the rent,
we're good.
(They will have to monitor me.)

Subatomic

Obeying some law but not all,
trapped in a force,
and in a reality she has little to do with.
A pretty particle that no one has,
not even that.

Hips

Thrusting,
walking,
further away,
further inside.

I Open

An actress,
another homeless,
defeated inside.

Deb

You are seriously going to have to do something about this.
I am psychically damaged.
He actually looked at me.

Pattern

I am stacks and stacks of man.
I see how simply it is put together.
A simple shape,
tiny,
repeated in stacks.
There are the down ones,

they blend together.
The up ones separate.
The down ones go inside.
The up ones branch out.

I Learned, I Learned, I Learned

That is when I was declared paranoid.
They said something special after break.
(It is brilliant, they only get willing answers; no one asking
for on the spot impressions, it eliminates that taint there.)
I thought someone would come in and cause a scene.
And then later, we would be asked to describe it,
be an eyewitness.
That was the depth of my knowledge of things.
I knew very little of psychological evaluation.
But that is what I expected. And I mentioned it.
How so many things get by you!
That must have been my fear—
missing things, details, important things.
I had rightly identified data-seeking.
But it's much more in depth.
"The ones who speak, what attacked their unknown?"
Mine was distrust of that unknown.
Attaching it to the nearest object.
Delusional distrust? A little bit.
Was there a group dynamic?
Was being a part of that a precipitating factor?
I can't see how. It was an organic reaction.
It was a very mild paranoia anyway.
A distrust of motives, that's all,
a really naïve distrust.

I learned a little bit about what being modern and
sophisticated really means though,
and that I was not it.
I must have presented quite a sight.

Willful

It is an outland crime,
there's a flyer posted somewhere.
It says this is what you must not be.
There is a feeling out there.
It is a blotting out instinct,
smashing out,
in a group preferably,
don't want to touch it too much—
there is haste, it is seen!

Private Eyes

Obsessively logical—more data, please.
Because there has to be, right?
What was she doing in 1997?
What was he in '93?
Gaps!
"I will give you a preliminary report.
I won't commit to anything."

Seconds

There they are!
Camped out in the foothills.
They lead up variously.
They obsessively blurt out what makes them hurt.

You may be smarter, have more knowledge,
but most of that is parsed out below you
in the foothills.
People can read that.
I am making my way up to you,
chatting with them along the way.

Not Guilty

Puppy dogs run away when yelled at.
They don't know yet they're trapped.
Eyes rolled up and frozen, that is not guilt from the adult.
It's just not the same thing.
Doctors say it's a playing dead defense mechanism.
It somehow survives in animals everywhere.
It's to be left dead.

You Are Not Like Me

It is a bolus correction,
or attempts to be.
It's an almost lethal dose.
Many, many side effects.
It's just stabilizing most of the time.

Hot

I'm sure no more fuss was made over your hair
or your makeup than usual, just the jacket.

Nice Poems

The one about your nightstand is coquettish.

It is also sad and old.

The flesh hominid is apparent.

But it is hard to understand—purposely hidden?

It goes far. It is acceptable.

I am plainer.

I would have to show you an erection instead.

Maintenance Class

You Are Loved

Try This

Go There

Cheer

Cry

Kroisos

I still can't get it out of mind

that you are just stripping down,

strolling out to the middle of the square,

and cutting your own throat for no good reason.

Boycott

A close up with blemishes—

I look at your eyes instead.

You've been crying.

No, almost crying.

I look at your lips and listen to what you're saying.

Then I don't.

Agreement

Moving forward with no regrets.
Tears cause waves.
This is no place to linger.

Fall Flat

It is what the writer thinks about me.
That is what is important.
There are gaps in his or her knowledge of me.
You look where there is.
In other words, where errors exist, look there.
That always reveals something.

Low Blow

I'd rather have a point taken off both our cards.
Have us both be in excruciating pain.
It is the most effective way.

Power

I see a huge fist punching
the face I just let in.
This together is strength.

Bad Opera

Technically trained and accurate,
just every emotion plastic,
not a real thing people feel,
not one of them.
No note in it is struck right.
And it cannot be adjusted post-production.

Three Hours

It is not often, it is always.
One cord is not working right.
If the range is 13, 14, 15, you are at 16 and 12,
all the time.
The other vocal cord is fine.

Become

Do you just go back home?
Just think about your next project?
You and *your* are deceiving here.
That has to be acknowledged.
Farmers used to go out to the field again,
that same day.
The son is dead.
Still the same old thing.

Pursuit

So we have a failed project.
The independent project that's followed,
it is mired, it is hopeless too.
The Movement needs new artists.
This opportunity fills the void.
It fills it completely.

Incomplete

These *Hail Marys* take five seconds
and then they're done.

Depression

What is the current research budget?
"Applications are now closed."
That is not encouraging.
Interns receive little pay, if any, just credit.
The paying chairs are all filled.
It's just their salaries on the clinical side.
They would probably go on for free.
There are network IT people involved too.
Most of these people can work anywhere by just saying hi.
There is no guilt in those layoffs.
That will free up some money.
Getting new people in for roles is clearly a challenge though.
Social activity and new people on the scene,
these two ingredients are what is needed to fill those positions.
But talk about social anxiety!
No one said this would be easy, non-stressful.

Smart Blender

Observe its hard, scratch resistant interior,
its molded design—
look how easy it is easy to store!
And it comes in a variety of colors.

Personalities

It takes a while for the egg to crack,
to give the outsiders a peek.
Dividing cellularity continues.
It can't properly be termed growth though.
The same size human gets divided.

Cognition

Signals are speciated.
All animals have detection systems.
This is the bad part of instinct.
Every kind of neural energy is dissipated into nature,
especially the red-lined, bioelectric release of panic.
I believe it is detected first, then affirmed in the eyes.
We conform our faces to it.
Birds fly down and look for themselves.
My presence reassures the blue jay.

Politburo

They come in early on Fridays to have their hydrotherapy.
Tuesdays they have sexual intercourse.
Their parenteral meals are twice a day.

Easy

Come on, don't make this hard; I am busy raising kids
and organizing a family.
Pay me well enough to go on vacation once in a while,
buy nice things,
and go out for beers sometimes.
I am not going to make a career out of this.
Don't make me even think about that!

Explosion

Just drive on back there on a four-wheeler,
take a look around.
It just takes a second, no one will know.
Then get the bomb.

Walk back there this time and bury it.
Set it off at the perfect time.

False

Some people do forget things,
block them out on purpose,
subconsciously.
Doesn't mean I do.
I would remember something like that.
You are mistaken. That was not me.
I did not get an invitation to that wedding.
That never happened.

Want

It becomes that?
Only if it's close.
Far away requires more,
two steps, three steps.

Valley of Death

The one in one hundred thousand will not be me.
That seems a reasonable mindset.
It's not my certainty from God.
I can't convince you or anybody of that.
It would be my job to convince you in another way.
At least this time it's simple.

Off Subject

I am not a protein source.

You know those King Kong vs Godzilla movies?
King Kong got stronger when electrified.
A big fucking monster gorilla going absolutely ape shit.

Hostess

Sweetened cherries,
the natural flavor
scientifically enhanced in so many ways.

Avant-Garde

If you're comfortable with that,
I guess I can't say anything more.
But there are times when I believe strange things,
say strange things,
and do strange things the culture finds unacceptable.

Miles

Clipped a million different ways,
but with a familiar pattern—
concerned discussions, blessed events, man and woman,
all this poured into us.
This is exactly who I am.
Some of us are completely out of that.
There is something there, but it's definitely not that.

Culture

This phenomena outside of me needs to be examined.
The concepts must be excised away from the flesh,
samples divided and microscopically examined.

Addendum

I'm sure a lot of cult leaders have seen themselves in songs,
as well as in the bible.
This is definitely the worst part of the whole thing.
It is the bloody part.
Nothing good can be said about it.
It is a slaughterhouse.
And it is the same song over and over 'til you're done.

Differential

I believe I am thinking right.
I also know I warned myself never to slip back
into thinking this way again.
I don't think I was ever convinced before.
Tried to avoid the subject.
If pressed, I wouldn't have denied it,
at least convincingly.

Interim

I must have said to myself at some point
in my coping
to not go further back,
not slip back into insanity.
Just hum the tunes.
What was the reason for that? Why hum?
It was to not see everything else.
The background noise would alter my perception.
I would be harder to fool.
That wouldn't help in customer service though.
Have to be a hundred percent focused.

No humming.
And it stopped kind of fading away.
It made me think of cool shit.
I purposely avoided actually hearing the songs.
Not the whole time,
I listened to some of the songs at the beginning.
There was nothing there though.
Just cool listening to them.
After I got my car, I fiddled back and forth,
but mostly settled on the public stations—
college music, classical music.
I didn't like the ads.
Did I feel manipulated?
The music would stop. And the suggestion would start.
I fled to the pledge drives instead,
and to things I never knew.
Talking to the people, it all returned,
the patterns appeared again,
the music and the television were dialogs again.

Radiotherapy

It is tempting to think of the cult-like
thing of music and religion
as the defense against the psycho-political intrusion.
I see people being censored. I feel it.
And I do respect psychological power.
I did, definitively, mix this power
with an evil, authoritarian state.
Why do so many people believe in things
that are so obviously wrong?
It gets an evil tinge.

In Situ

It annoys me and I rebel against it.
To be buried in your arms, then,
where there are no more amplified voices—
there, my mind imagines suffocation,
I can't go there.

Stage 1

Raising of the arms in victory for two minutes is supposed
to somehow help self-confidence.
That was confronting me.
There out of nowhere.
This might start getting weird.

Iago

The dominant ones seem the least able to handle it.
They just have to be in charge.
Oh, it never goes away.
One of them will make the right choice eventually
and win.
The logical usually requires a little doing.
This requirement eliminates a lot of people immediately.
There is a whole lot of luck involved too.
This eliminates the rest.
All except the one.
You have to come up with a timeline first.
How long will this take?
If, after coming up with that,
an emergency pops up requiring immediate action
early in this time frame,

you have no choice but to be more ruthless and violent
than later in the game.
Better off not victorious. An escape is optimal,
but each choice has to remain logical,
victory is one of those options you sometimes have to take.

Sub-Basement

Starting from today,
it's just an elevator ride down,
a fast elevator--
it will stop,
it will stop,
it will stop!

Seize

The reflection jiggles.
I am convulsing.
It gives an illusion of rage,
a striking down,
a guilty.

Plea

I feel like I've yelled loudly.
And I have a chance at mercy
O God!
But now I have to whimperingly explain.

Beautiful

You used to be nice,

now you crawl.
You desire.

Seller

This is the book that will put me over the top.
I feed off the bewitched.
I am truly low class.

Possessed

You are experiencing something totally unique
in the universe.
It is impossible to resist.
No, with help, there is a chance.
It will always be there, even so.
The radio, the television, movies,
they will have to be avoided.
Go hiking, the gym.

Lower Class

Everything is so nice and tidy.
This irritates me.
I am all appendages,
and squeezed in.
I can't stop talking when it's us.
If more, I can't.
I notice all the flaws around me.
Then I forget.
I drop things and pick them up.
Why do I drop things?

Line Prompting

I wonder what happens?
Will there be a play button?
Will it be the same as now?
Will I even remember now?
There is nothing to remember—
the documents!

Cave

I wonder if she's looking?
No way she's not.
Sometimes there's no escape,
a lot of the time.
She has to see it coming.

Not Progress

It may make more rocket ships,
but isn't this just a bunch of nuts
shooting off bottle rockets on a hill?
That is what it'll start to look like.

I'm Splitting

I am someone else.
So many faults.
Not enough good things.
This cannot be dealt with.
I was made by myself.
I am someone else.

Mechanism

They are right. She is right.
There really isn't one good thing,
nothing.
I want a Mounds Bar,
sweet coconut and chocolate,
and licorice.

Cheater

Uh oh, she's reading the report,
all the details.
There's the flash drive,
all the photos, video, and recordings.

Parrots

I skin-walk into people.
If they knew, they'd freak.

Views

I will give in,
hide behind the trees,
peek,
I am fascinated.
Some good, some bad,
enough diversity to enforce conformity.

Potty

I will wait for her outside the restroom—
I am at the fair, I just noticed.

A lot of people are here,
it smells,
it's hot,
I am sunburned.
Maybe I should go.

A Sensitive

She is susceptible to this information, and it comes.
She will not search for it, it comes.
She is not a part of it.
The deer, the tyrannosaurus, they are part of it.

Reputation

All will be ready tomorrow—
oh wait, I forgot the passport.
No. it's here.
It will be cool working with her.

NSA

I know something…
It's a deep secret.

Privat

I know someone is monitoring me.
It is you.

Place

Exhaust fans, pipes, sunny days,
backs and sides of buildings,

fronts too,
there's always an exact reason why everything is there.
The regulars, as well, why they come and go,
why they stay.
Anyone else in the picture prevents the logical flow of it.
That's why the lines are painted there,
that's why the signs.
It can be cloudy, but it cannot rain; rain gives
everybody problems.

Personal Growth

If the farmer times his crops
with stars
and multiples of seven,
and accomplishes things,
it is a valid way of thinking.
I would press the *I don't really care* button
on most of your corrections.
It is my job to produce art.
Wrong instinctual thoughts go into some of it, I'm sure.
I think I do a good job with most of it,
accuracy and so forth,
I don't think you want to mess with it.

That Thing

She rides a bike.
She totally ignores me.
She looks really good in spandex.

Graveyard

They are mostly cleaned and swept,
the places I find least comfortable—
unless I've done it.
Then anxious and proud,
morphing into a steady state.

Hawaii

Acres and acres of beachfront property,
screen door humming,
studying sleeping eyelids.

Squaresville

You live in a closed society.
Then you come to this atomic conclusion,
divide the day from the night,
tap instinct instead of pride.
Here is a keenness, a drive.
It is cultivated, shaped, kneaded,
squeezed into oblivion, and then remade.
It never takes more than a *ghostly* form though.
You are a stranger,
an act without a will.
Add beats, add words, dance floor—
we are papers somehow drifting in the streets,
right at dawn,
in a deserted downtown.
This is before you wake up.

Talk

This carries with it the death penalty.

I can see, now, that this is bigger than all of you.
It is the tide and the moon.
Protesting my humanity will only lose my teeth,
and I'll suffocate in gags.
Maybe that's a solace.
A phantom though, if you can handle it, is the way to go.

Doctor Erotic

I put my t-shirt on first because I know
how much that annoys you.
Like any medicine, its intended effect becomes blunted
by reiteration
and the aging process.
But that anger, even mixed with everything else,
still works perfectly well.
I am pleased with its effects.
And I am getting used to the occasional remarks.

Carnival

Tell them!
Tell them!
There won't be any magic!
There won't be any magic.
See?
That's better.
We can walk right over there.
They won't bother us.
And there is no magic!

Age of Aquarius

If I just keep the wine light,
there will be less ruined nights.
And plaid, stop wearing plaid!

Frontal Lobes Swimming

I throw myself into the online data stream.
I customized my tone for singles and multiples of ten.
It Geigers in the morning and hums in the afternoon.

OB

I listen, instead of music now,
to other vital things.
These sounds together are the new factor.
A chipset has been added to the process.
I added lights to be reminded,
they flash red and blue.

Empty Quiet

Secret people look through secret walls.
They monitor the unstable.
They are the ones who barely function.
They are the ones for which the past and the future
are just too massive.

Summer Vacation

A plane or a lawnmower,
the clovers smell nice,
bees, bugs, grass, fences, rocks,
there are no streets,

it is all backyard and hot
with cool breezes.
In the morning, the ridges seem to go on and on,
and they seem populated even through a mist.
In the afternoons, they seem empty even with the birds,
even with the haze.
It is not clover, it is the grass next door,
or a couple of houses away.
Warmer breeze now,
with radio, peat, and moss.
All of them baking
and crusting
aloft.

Tanks

Fast horses would be an absolute terror
in the future world
when the gas runs out
and people try to build things.

Germs

The witches in the woods,
the caves,
they are the remnant after we die.
They go through their own paces,
stud themselves,
run along the hillsides,
continually circle,
can bolt in any direction,
can rampage and stomp.

Basic Code

The practiced howls
through the endless beatings
were produced from the love
that only the end of things can bring.
A communication through the lungs, through the throat—
a communication!

Cold Blooded

You wonder why I'm paranoid!
Who comes up with this shit?
How do you sleep at night?
Dropped.
Bloody as hell here!
This is terrible!
Blood all over the place!
And brains!

Being Known

Constantly leave clues, you know,
that you know you are being watched.
Buy *Catcher in the Rye* all the time.
And routinely go to places you don't normally go.

Verdict

The vote was unanimous as usual;
no one is insane.

Sentence

This survivor has built himself up.
He is the strong man here.
These things have to be stomped out.

Scored

A weather vane on sale at Home Depot!
I don't care what it costs,
I don't care where it's from,
it's some kind of metal,
I don't care,
I am buying it.

Fool

Death is a group of people,
a romantic situation,
a confrontation,
layer upon layer every day.

Me v. My

My reasoning eye takes in more.
Its judgment, *impossible*.
And it sends that impulse into my bones.

Peace

Have some fucking respect!
Show some courtesy!
This is not a joke!

Option 1

I tend to ignore the idiots.
Others bully them, and bully them, and bully them.
That is a hate affair.

Option 2

Mean is real.
The way I feel in its presence is real too.
I cannot go away.
I deal with it the best can.
I (real) limit my experience with it (real).

Lessen

I am not going to be manipulated by you
or anyone else.
I deal with liars all day long.
There are techniques to discover them,
though they mostly reveal themselves,
they are so proud.

Manifesto

It is a current of black ink,
printed sixty pages long.
I have blood circulating in my veins.
That is a biohazard.

Intimacy

You're busy kicking ass all day,
online business, lunches, dinners, psychotherapy.
Then there are the ones who open doors.

They don't go very far in.
They know where each one of them is though.

Optim

Businesses have departments.
They have directors.
Goals are set.
Good people are sought.
They are mentored.
Everybody makes money.

Little Guy

I let the dog out.
He will come back in.
I think I've built them high,
dug them deep,
the fences.

Full Reports

"Two advisors in each ear,
two in theirs—this won't work.
I want to discuss your delusions, but hold on,
I am getting an earful.
(I will ask for a full report this. They are good at that.)"

Ulcer

The wise just stay silent about it. The tenured
give it praise. The wound stays open,
ignored and adored. Sometimes gets better,

sometimes gets worse.

AM Radio

The morning is sober.
The buzzing of, *I don't care anymore, I'm doing it*,
is sleeping now.
Let's find a nice cup of coffee somewhere.

Teacher

This is the law.
I will teach you all about it.
This still goes through my mind.
Even staring at other people's faces,
and seeing them clearly.

Hi All

This is Matthew from the National Office.
Susan and Jonas apologize for this sudden announcement,
but they will no longer be directing this chapter.
All workflow will now be managed through my office.
I have spearheaded the turnarounds in our Tacoma chapter
and Gig Harbor. It is thought that my methods will prove
fruitful here as well.
I have sent each Member of the team confidential information
regarding an internal matter. You will receive this later today.
You will also receive information regarding a new application.
This will be in the same email, as the two things are related.
I think each Member of my staff needs to know as much as
possible about the data breach. I think it is essential for the
growth of the Seattle office.

I look forward to communicating with you.

Matthew,

Manager
Community Relations, Puget Sound Region / Optilan
/ Box ##### / Seattle, WA. #####-###
Cell: ###-###-#### / Email: ####@##.###

*"Incompetence with some dashes of cowardice
and legal paralysis, that is what caused all this." J.*

*The information in the above email is personalized for each
Member of the team. Its content is on a need to know basis.
Do not discuss it in any way with anyone.*

Andrew

I want you to familiarize you with a few details concerning a situation that occurred in our Texas Hill Country Region. A programmer named David had concealed an application in the Austin chapter's Optilan system. This was recruiting software that he was contracted to develop. Unbeknownst to the company, David was utilizing the software in an unauthorized manner. And this was before the company even knew that the product was complete.

Within a short time, David was able to amass hundreds of followers within the company worldwide. And this was just using the application he developed, nothing else. But these people followed David and not the company. This was stopped on December 17 of last year.

Since then, we have recycled all of David's work.

Yarn

And it is now being used for its intended purpose—
to recruit new Members.
Jason has been pleased with the way my office has
transformed our unhealthy chapters using this application.
We both look forward to working with you to transform
the Seattle chapter.
The application has been loaded onto your terminal as of today.
Log in as you normally would. You will notice 40 accounts
in your work queue. These are dummy accounts that we
are asking you to work for the next 10 days. Normal
production will be 25 new accounts per day. That begins
March 1. That is the go live date. And we all expect you
to be up to speed by then. Please familiarize yourself
with each aspect of the software. The chat box has two
operators available, AL and LEO. Each of these are absolutely
essential sources for the everyday accounts you will be given
beginning March 1. You will follow their instructions to the letter.

Matthew,

Manager
Community Relations, Puget Sound Region / Optilan
/ Box ##### / Seattle, WA. #####-###
Cell: ###-###-#### / Email: ####@##.###

*"All of the lost are at our mercy. The humane treatment
of all of them has not changed." J.*

*The information in the above email is personalized for each
Member of the team. Its content is on a need to know basis.
Do not discuss it in any way with anyone.*

PTO

I have a 104 degree temperature.

Matthew,

Manager
Community Relations, Puget Sound Region / Optilan
/ Box ##### / Seattle, WA. #####-###
Cell: ###-###-#### / Email: ####@##.###

"All these heads of Armageddon are the historical enemies of Israel." J.

The information in the above email is personalized for each Member of the team. Its content is on a need to know basis. Do not discuss it in any way with anyone.

Current Trouble

All the things that are happening now have to be put into perspective. We are just simple individuals. The complex of machines that decides everything is the one that is confused. Since we absolutely depend on this system, I think it has to figure it all out. I mean, right?

Matthew,

Manager
Community Relations, Puget Sound Region / Optilan
/ Box ##### / Seattle, WA. #####-###
Cell: ###-###-#### / Email: ####@##.###

"I am doing everything possible to prevent people from dying out there in the streets. Everything." J.

The information in the above email is personalized for each Member of the team. Its content is on a need to know basis. Do not discuss it in any way with anyone.

Leadership Message

What else is there to say? Everybody is dead and I am abandoned. I just hear footsteps running down the hallways really fast. I even hear them on the streets through these windows, really fast.

Matthew,

Manager
Community Relations, Puget Sound Region / Optilan
/ Box ##### / Seattle, WA. #####-###
Cell: ###-###-#### / Email: ####@##.###

"Away from instead of next to, what does that mean? Concentrate on the positive part of the phrase, away from." J.

The information in the above email is personalized for each Member of the team. Its content is on a need to know basis. Do not discuss it in any way with anyone.

No Subject

Why were they visible?

Manager
Community Relations, Puget Sound Region / Optilan
/ Box ##### / Seattle, WA. #####-###
Cell: ###-###-#### / Email: ####@##.###

"It is the living that haunt the dying, not the dead." J.

The information in the above email is personalized for each Member of the team. Its content is on a need to know basis. Do not discuss it in any way with anyone.

Unbalanced

There is an actual ledger!
Paranoia grows very quickly.
This is a bumper crop!
And the state farms these
beautifully.
Acres and acres of them.

Fill In

What am I doing here?
I am not original or unique enough to fit in.
I don't know enough people.
This issue makes me angry, _____.
Great, I am definitely in the wrong place.

The Blank

No.
Look at this…
This is what I want to change, _____.

I said no.

Cryptid

They come down to grasp
the one who doesn't seem to understand.
"This is how love is supposed to be felt."
He hides.
It is a desperate attempt to contribute to the positive
by becoming a null.

Cemented

I hope you overheard, and understood,
when I commented on others wearing orange,
or told people what my favorite color was.

On My End

I'm sorry, I'm simpleminded, I guess.
I will try to understand you.
I wonder if you will do the same for me?
There is some other thing *like* what's going on.
Paint or write, *it* comes out.
It is not what's going on.
It is a lie in that sense.
It is up to me make sure only in that sense.
Change? How is that actualized?
I try to describe *this*,
I cross out a word,
and it becomes *that*,
a completely different concept,
and I go on a riff about *that*.

I tried to paint it,
I see the real image below it,
it becomes that,
and I finish it that way.
Was it stopped? The original intent?
Is there a satanic element to it?
"Here is a lie. Try this."
There is an influence in it,
secret knowledge, revelation, that jazz.
That moral, theme, philosophy, position
permanently changes in me though,
that is my point.
And this happens just because of *that*.
A psychoanalytic result, if you like.
My person is self-created in this way.

Your End

He is a missionary. His name is Chung.
He absolutely believes in the Leader.
He absolutely loves and has gotten used to
fine living and an expense account.
He is the type of man this situation produces.
He knows he's being watched, and he's perfect.
Sometimes he doesn't play his roles right.
In which case he completely abandons them,
abruptly.
That is protocol.
Most of the time he is spot on.
95%.
He is a beast of burden who's learned to read the human face.
He knows what to say.

He has a trained, rehearsed, memorized mind.
He knows what to do.
In his checkups, lately, all the docs wear masks.
This is a mistake.
He tells me he feels uneasy about this. Like,
suddenly,
it's up to him.
"This is retirement?"
He is smart.
"What would they have me do? Getting old is bad."
I proposed that he take it as a working hypothesis
that it is euthanasia,
some kind of 21st century version of it.
"How does freedom equal death?"
Half true, knowledge of freedom.
Kim is a soldier. He lives alone.
He kills people all the time.
Chung tries to help Kim.
They are not observed communicating.
Chung doesn't even spy him out.
He says he does that to me all the time.
They communicate solely by the code.
They talk about sexuality frankly,
they talk about their health problems,
dreams, mothers, socialism.
All three of us agree that this is a natural thing,
circumstances brought all of this together,
there is no unseen hand.
And it is all honest communication; we are all very naïve,
that adds to the honesty.
Kim hates everyone.
He does pushups and pullups constantly.

He runs the treadmill nude.
He runs it fast.
He knows what everyone in his building is doing at
all times.
Chung says Kim doesn't understand the concept
of being a racketeer.
He mentioned to him a famous actor in the news once
who played gangsters a lot,
and he totally didn't know what he was talking about.
He thinks it's just codes, working out, details in reports,
and killing.
I don't think either of them understand the concept
of being a racketeer.
And I think neither one of them ever gets distracted.
There is a compulsion. The higher ups must see that.
I have never felt so compelled to open an envelope
as I did for Chung's that first day.
I actually felt my arm become a wolfman's.
I somehow cannot look for him.
I just can't.
I never look at anyone anymore like I used to.
Just who's in front of me, someone necessary.
I think it's so fucked up that people like that exist.
What they do and that they're doing it to me,
so fucked up.

Usual Suspects

This series of plinks
results in a candidate
being vetted,
99% guaranteed.

The computer
can predict these
just by age,
and college,
and known contacts.
The successful candidate
is never not on that list.

Down Time

The indigo light reflects up
from underneath the door.
I will wait.
Central Park is there. I see the indigo light reflected
in the window too.
There are people wandering around in jeans down there.
They are always in couples too.
"Oh, the housekeeper is here. Got everything?"

Waste

Dig! Displace that dirt, Bruno!
Through the legs and out the back door.
Throw a little dirt on them,
and never give them a second thought.

Fear!

It incorporates.
It unsophisticates.
It panics.
It ruins.
It kills.

It runs over.

Lipizzan

Horses are broken.
The masks leave out a vital piece of information.
Is it up to me, again?
Then I'll just throw your ass to the ground!
Let's see…what's next?
Oh shit! The whip!
I'm depressed.

Driving Support Systems

Just because you can make a self-driving car,
doesn't mean you can make a self-driving human.
That is a good foundational approach.
Forward thinkers are just as behind as everyone else on this.
You are in the breakables section of the human.
I really do appreciate not crashing into things with my car,
but there are people who really know about these things.
I don't think positronic circuits will work.
That's a low opinion of humanity.
We battle.

Present

Scrambling up out of the spaghetti, a killer awakes.
A tickled ear, a time to check out,
a hold on, an all physical laws in abeyance,
Edward J. Hominid here.

For Sale

A '65 Buick nothing car
painted six years ago
black.
It is on somebody's brown farm,
their acre,
dead grandpa's.

Critically Endangered

There is hardly anyone left in the city.
The gas stations look so shiny.
You would think
the roads would be absolutely full of traffic jammed cars,
and the gas stations jammed with cars and skeletons.
The whatever businesses,
the ones with no landscaping,
so crisp,
the A/C is still working.

Business Plan

That is what you have to do,
make something as small as possible when compact,
so when not,
fragile
and easily breakable.

Just That?

That's nothing compared to other things I've done.
I am in the artistic community, the real one.
I've done a lot of better stuff than that.

One

Like a cool guy moves,
he's always been like that
even if it's just been a week.
It's cerebral,
encased in the hard skull—time?

Rotate

Gravity misses and there is revolution,
falling inward and missing.
People shouldn't know this,
it gets into the moods.

Venus Rising

Surely no one will know we are there.
I will be very discreet.
The mountains are far away, but I can go there too.
I can even climb them.
Rise early and sneak away.
Recline and beam, cast shadows.

Battery Mode

One guy will have left at four a.m. or something,
and the spot will have remained empty since then.
I am rolling on almost completely silent; this lot must have
been swept and power washed.
The lines are freshly painted, and it is freshly dewed,
lovely patterns of domes on the oil-based white.
There is a robin eating a worm,
a mouse venturing out of the bushes,

I am interrupting.
I do hear a garbage truck five blocks away.
The wind is blowing zero miles an hour.
There are wispy clouds on the horizon.

No Function

Units and sections shutting down,
a dimming of illumination at night,
a dying town.

Daytime

Why do you watch me?
It is sick.
And it's just questions?
In your files, enter blah blah blah.

Mayday

The rage spreads to the populace.
The pathway of least resistance
chooses someone, say, homeless…

Wind

We find people that get online and threaten.
They find people that make their skin crawl.
They accuse them of crimes
that someone like them
might possibly have committed.
They give examples of violence and retribution.

Rain or Shine

Sprinklers will go on soon.
They will rattle, spittle, burp to life.
They will make something already lush, paradise.
Flowers out of nowhere.

Station Break

*Tonight at eight, T.J. Hooker tracks down the crazed
bank robbers who kidnapped his adopted daughter.*
Those perps are going to die.

Complex

There is a pond with frogs,
there is a wetland almost all the way around,
it is hilly,
there are footbridges,
there are stairs.
It is lush.
No matter how many things they put in here,
how much concrete is poured in,
trees grow up and out of it, and grass,
and whatever else they plant.
They are happy.
The tangled roofs slope up proud,
all painted the same.
The units are squared off at right angles rimming the edges.
A hiker built this,
saw buildings in the stones.
Or a pilot,
saw grids.

The giant pine trees a half a block away are the watchers.
The non-pine trees in the wetland sway in the wind.
Sometimes they walk a bit in the slosh,
but it is right now,
they are locked in for the Spring.
Not even a thunderstorm moves them.
They are cemented in.
Until November, at least.

Someone Yelled

Someone just went out into the middle part,
the courtyard,
and yelled something.

Redacted

Where did I go?
Did I leave?
I was supposed to be somewhere, and I wasn't.
I was…
I don't remember.
I saw an ambulance.
It was stopped in front of me.
I went inside.

Induction

You are going to have a hard time convincing
anyone that logic isn't hampered by nature.
It gets totally in the way.
To fine tune it, logic has to be sequestered.
What more proof do you need?

Taste

Our consumer-hominid travels miles for this banana.
Others partake of the stack in the cage.

Underdog

That person has everything, I have nothing.
That boiled-down brain comes up with some good shit.
There's a lot of hate down there, have to be careful.
Success completely ruins this. Completely.
The censors keep this community flourishing.

Outburst

I am not qualified to comment on that.
Any word on it would only have a negative effect—
on me,
on everyone.
I want it put in the record
that I was asked what I thought about something
that I had no power or duty to comment on.
It was not a refusal to answer.
It was an objection to an improper question.
The hearing was not dismissed,
I have the right to object to a question.

Clunker

I heard a really loud car going up the hill just now.
Had to stop at lights—what bad luck!
Wonder where it's going?
4 AM.
Planned for the middle of the night?

Less cars on the road, less eyes.
But where?
Probably to a park.

Ad Hominem

It is a logical argument on whether
he or she is a good person,
not logical on what he or she said.
You are going to have a different argument for that.
The subject and predicate of the thought spoken,
that is what is at issue.
Berger's objection would be sustained as
incompetent and irrelevant.
The first part because it is a classical logical fallacy,
one of the biggies,
and has to be mentioned first.

Case Dismissed

The meeting on this should last about 15 seconds.
The court rules the accusations lack any merit.
Any more time spent on it would be harassment.

House Rules

I am better at this job in some things, way better.
And she's the same with me, in way more ways.
We help each other out to help the team.
I don't see how that is not teamwork.
We are not Navy Seals on a tactical mission; no lives
are at stake.
If we're deemed to be at fault for this behavior,

I'm sure both of us will oblige.
I abide by laws I don't understand all the time,
I need this job.
I need this corner of civilization to nestle in.
This outweighs anyone I happen to be communicating with
in there.

That Salesman

It was a two syllable word,
Corbett, Rupert, some almost extinct first name.
I was reading *Babbitt* at the time.
J,
Je,
Jean,
I can see his face saying, "Jean".
He said he was a certain nationality.
French?
He said he had to go through his father's books again.
He had the rights.
That book could make a million!
Jean, French, teeth, eyes, tongue—
I just sat there and listened to him.
I wasn't going to buy any of his shit.
I would remember his name when he would come in,
I would flash on it,
push play.
L,
Lloyd?
S?
When you say a name like his,
it is instantly forgettable.

Like he wants it to be
after he's taken everything you have.
And I mean everything, his lusts were extreme.
People were impressed that I remembered his name
when I did.
I remember him being shocked.

Lawrence

Is Javier gone yet? Back to the east coast? Not sure?
Oh man, he is a genius.
That app thing is the greatest idea ever.
He will make a hundred million.
The DBT thing—I got to get his number.
I know about these things.
I was in intelligence for twenty years.
I've kept up on it.
My dad was in it too.
He wrote a book on it.
All those methods are 100% valid.
And the app makes it even better.
He's probably better off getting all the money himself.
He would have labs all over the planet.
They would come up with some shit.
Tell him I'm looking for him.

Pleasured

His father wanted to name him Lee Harvey Oswald.
His dad won salesman of the year five times in a row.

Fragile

However it has happened, I am happy.
It is the extreme danger time.
I am between the onset and the rescue.

Blind Date

So rainy and such a shitty car,
no AAA,
got my phone—
hope she doesn't live out in the woods.

Things Seen

The hominid DNA we share
has a glimmer in it
that can develop a toleration
for a few dozen dead bodies.
In the major cities,
tens of thousands,
the smell—
reason would give up this fight.
After getting those few hundred every day,
there will be absolutely nothing done about it,
and they will pile.

Threat

You have been rebuked.
You can either continue with the behavior,
dismissing the rebuke,
or stop the behavior.
God made people, so God hardened hearts.
It will be hard to get on Spaceship Jesus

and escape the bloodbath.

Famine

And the priests of the internet,
they will become the power.
Locked away and kept alive to keep the internet going.
Otis must be allowed to live-stream eating grandpa,
the one he caught trying to fly away in his Prius.
Every single scrap of animal is gone.
Just tiny birds every once in a while.
Everyone has nets.
There are no harvests because of violence.
There is nothing to eat.

Baseball Cards

How long did it take to memorize the baseball uniforms?
And the football and basketball?
Maybe two years. I was seven.
That age,
67 different teams,
I must have used shortcuts.
Sorting them leads to sorting them quicker—
visual cues, hand-eye,
new definitions of color that can't be expressed.
The quality, statistics of them,
were played around with later in childhood.
The qualities of the individuals?
There were names then,
that's not quite the same thing.
I don't think I judged their ugliness.
The oldness of some of the managers jarred me a little.

Faustus D Program

When you hear about hackers, sometimes
the target was just one certain file.
Blow up the internet for just that one thing.
Go in, do it, and remove all evidence.
Paranoia is everywhere.

Otto Cannotbe

Who is Nemesis?
Ever admire yourself?
When it is denied in return.

Illicit

I kind of figured the lovey-dovey stuff
was out of the question.
Dutiful staff member, that seemed the best.

Folded Into

Pumpkin pie, no whipped cream,
an orange thing organized,
it felt good under my skin,

Not an arrow;
no one turns in that direction.

Many

Why the same?

It seems more reasonable to be more than one.
Even the boring ones like this seem nicer.
We don't waste our different.
Ourselves will always be plentiful.
From all others is not our goal.

Too Many

Let it die! Hide that canvas!

You Are Ugly

No way someone good looking is after me.
But why would I think that?
It's not for the physical pleasure of it, the fantasy.
I'm not denying that's there, but it doesn't begin the thought.
Some attribute that stands out that is worthy of affection?
The person does not like me. The person likes this.
This projects shallowness on the beholder,
but it fits in nicely with my negative view of things.
And it frees me from much of the responsibility
of respecting it.
I am free to seek other affection, as well,
and with the same bait!
All these negative terms!
This is just hominid nature.
It is bad!

PRN

Water doesn't exist.
Nothing does except this migraine.
Put the tablet in your mouth and drink the water.

The water and the tablet have a marginal existence then.
Nothing like a prescription!

Brand of Cheese

The creative has a community contract.
Cited misinterpretation is a human right.
And it is for the simple reason that it might be right.
Maybe the original source misspoke.

Supine

That is Jekyll, Hyde fallen,
an empty liar after all.
But I give a bad impression,
even counting all the Twitter nonsense,
the people I am talking about
are never old news.

Assistant

Cursive was designed to help you write faster.
And shorthand after that.
Hear what someone is saying and write it down.
This is so you don't forget.
Then tape recorders.
Someone just doesn't have time to repeat themselves
or go through things more slowly—
you've got to get this, blah, blah, blah.

Up to Speed

Just fulfil the requirement of brevity, that seems to be

the one goal.
The level of competence this brings is negative,
a downward trend.
It becomes a free fall with high turnover.
Somehow, through all this, numbers still reach production.

The Crisis

You are the insecure one. I will wait for your mistake.
Where is that usually made?
What do I need to get? A big thing? A little thing?
Don't want too much, I have to remember that,
just what I need, this leaves less stress for me.
Easier to figure out how you're going to give it to me.

The Consultants

When someone comes up with a solution to something,
it implies previously working on it.
The more complex a problem, the less likely an outsider
can come and fix it.
Outsiders might have the ability to get people to buy in,
i.e., leadership,
and that is the quality they look for under them—
it does create a beautiful photo gallery
with great bios.
Between the lines of their solutions though,
we will read about the actual problems addressed,
the ones that have nothing to do with anything,
and a *what the hell are they talking about* will follow.

The Altogether

The glass corridor to the exit,
the entry on the other side,
there should be a place to sit down,
even crouch down in.
I have no t-shirt on, bare-chested.
I asked for one from someone I used to know.
Didn't mind the no.
Dark stairwells, lighted stairwells—fraternization going on.
I don't know where I am going.
Just go in one, go down a floor,
find another one,
go up a few, find another open floor,
find another stairwell,
and go down there—
exit door and it is cold outside.
I am making it. It is almost deserted.
Early enough for traffic—still people are seeing me!

The Corpse

Existence ends, I don't.
My intellect cannot conceive of this,
I will reach across,
I will commune with you,
I will say I love you over and over.
Do not wear a robe,
it reminds me of judges.
Do not wear a suit either.

That Part Apart

Unsustained,
  owned,

left,
unread.

Gallery

Still lifes, colors, contours—
it is different though, individualized somehow.
Then I see a portrait that has that same effect.
Then I wonder about that human I see.

Voices

There was also the thing about the dead guy,
and whether he wanted people to do things.
That question hurt her.
I told her the dead person didn't want anything.
She still scheduled a novena.

Networking

The fire department cleanup crew
that I was introduced to last week,
their lead was at the party.
And we went to the sites the next day.
I was just in the way in both places.
And there were people talking to themselves.

Tex

I saw his horse at the bar. He didn't know it was gone.
What must he think of me?
I just met him,
and here I am telling him I just saw his horse at the bar.

He didn't even know it was gone.
But he doesn't seem to be giving the situation
a second thought.

Corny

When something's been done a thousand times,
been done ten thousand times,
it doesn't mean it's become bad.
Cool things happen that way too,
and never get old.

Plain

I am just trying to accomplish the objective of the plan.
I know I am a subhuman on the streets. Can't accomplish
much out there.
Maybe in another way.

COD

Because he was a fucker!
There's your reason!

Same Beaming

You could say it's like plugging in,
charging,
the collection phase of solar power.
The electric current in the outlet
is pretty much exactly the same every time.
It tastes the same.

Hard Reflections

Whatever that thing is, it is not the opposite of selfish.
It's about as different as can be, but not opposite.
I do not think I am good enough
for just about anything
or anyone.
That's a fact.
He takes up almost everything
except the selfish prick part.
A lot of times I think I'm really better
than a lot of people.
Do you think that progression to the prick
has an analogous expression to the subhuman?
Not opposite conditions, just two very different ones.

Creep

There are times when I have to convince myself
that I am funny.
I know I am ugly but not repulsive.
I have to convince myself of that too.
It's not bi polar or depression, doctor.
Reality drives a tunnel through this thought matrix—
repulsive and stupid.
I am funny,
how can that be a part of it?

Gotcha

Being so naïve as to fall for something so simple—
just follow the law, there will be no problem, have an ethic.
Selfish takes what it doesn't deserve.

Live by the law, die by the law.
Your only creative acts, tricks.

Person-To-Person

It is your insight into behavior modification that has merit.
The art that you create is good too.
Your theory on music is delusional.
Your fake life is bad fiction.
They come together, at least for me.
The music and the fake life came before and are tolerated.
It is just a relapse.
It somehow gets out and spreads though.
Because it is unique? The story?
It has to be more than that.
The thoughts, the music, and the fake life,
they were already there—dormant? Growing?
The surplus of energy had to be released; and so it was
in my art and my persona.
Like anxiety, it has physical manifestations.
I keep it in for art. Try.

Smear

You are all being fucked!
There is no secret life, no alter-ego.
The evidence is fabricated!

Weirdo

I know I do the opposite sometimes on purpose.
But most of the time it just happens that way.
Yes, that proves there is something in my bones.

Sometimes there is coincidental circumstance
that make it appear that way too.
Things that are not only not conscious,
but not a part of me at all.
Like why I went to the bookstore the day he was killed.
That had nothing to do with anything.

Voluntary?

I am not going to do anything that would cripple my life
on purpose.
There would have to be a strong reason for an exception
to that rule.

Geppetto

"The world is changing,
and with a populace less capable of handling it mentally,
we have to use behavior modification."
It's the other things you do, not just that.
It is the nothing culture you are creating.

High Voltage

You will get locked up saying that
about the little darlings.
Try to mouth the drivel
and be pointy at the same time.

Very Definition

You don't think that's negative?
Provoked or otherwise,

of course it is.
Denying that proves your stupidity on the subject,
or your delusional thinking.
Can't even get to first base with you.

Bingo

Every nerve fired.
A magnetic field too.
Don't touch him!
Turn off the power.

Blown Out

In rare years, I happen, a higher place.
That is how it's supposed to be.
That is our instinct weakness.
Warped space gives us a view of Nirvana.
Perpetual motion there too.

A & M

Grassroots? Are the blades dead?
No, just not fed enough.
What chemical compounds are needed for photosynthesis?
Got plenty of the photo.
The soil needs to be hydrated and fertilized.

Important

That thing will be there too.
What?
Details, details…

Rockin

God is not on my side.
Things are not going my way.
Down the list,
I am not special, attractive,
no one has plans for me,
no one is testing me (that's a good thing).
I am a dirty little man who repels.

Public Eyes

I can't read it.
It has to be obsessive,
and nobody's with that with me.

GI Tract

Oily hairs pick up debris,
debris that might include harmful organisms.
The cows tail constantly whipping, like that.
As for my beard, the debris is picked up and whisked away.
A forest canopy, dark and warm, that's good too.

New Car

I'm not used up.
I am a brand new Prius.
Power flows to and from the battery all the time.
The engine is in perfect condition.
Interior clean.
All the latest gadgets available.

Cult

The insipid is spreading.
Give up all you have,
and at the same time make things worse for everyone else.
Most of us,
we just watch and keep our mouths shut.
Made up our minds millennia ago.
No one needs to know our decision.
People in the public eye,
they are forced.
They are sad.
And even sadder when they're genuine.

Quagmire

This should work!
It has compiled zero errors!
A working model at least!
Seems everything just works the opposite!

Diagnostic Report from Space

Logic prepares the facts,
the communications center has access to the emotions—
you speak, you act.
That is not it.
It is a state of mind that is not expressed,
it stay interior—
it flares up every once in a while—
that is it.
(The selfish part is because you're a dick.)

Failure

You're thinking it's some kind of novice phobia,
well it's not.
Could it have started there? Like a pre-condition?
There's something deeper.
I am not the same as you, lesser.
Things that are good in themselves
do not include socializing.
An affirmation of inclusion is not attainable for me.
If it makes someone happy
with whom I have a chance of inclusion,
well then
things can go from there.
That has the key ingredient of being a point.
That usually pisses people off, knowing that though.
And that could lead to a crisis element being added to things,
novice phobia does come into picture then,
you can practice your medicine when that happens.

High Class

That is so first grade.
I got plenty of stars back then too.
Then I fit in and stopped caring.
I'm not going to be taken to school.
Whatever your score is will have to do.
Astronomical victories get old after a while.

Butter Top Icing

Honey, this time make it cinnamon spice
body lotion that you rub into your thighs.

Mate

I saw that dress before.
(I don't want this to be a dialog.)
(I want this to be a dialogue.)
I have that other personality in mind.

Serious People

I am caught up in the rackets,
a scrambling entrepreneur,
a no experience, dumb guy.
I have just lost someone's money and it is gone.
There is no chance of getting it back.
I'm in debt myself.
I have a family, I can't run.
Or can I?
There is no way out.
Call old friends in the old life, two years ago,
see if anything's up,
something on the ground floor,
a high-end, big profit type thing.
Maybe that can be used to negotiate a settlement.
No, it has to be drug related.
Maybe others are like me.
I can break thumbs.
Get in on the ground floor there. Be protected too.
Can deal on an even level.
Can explain at least that it wasn't my fault,
that I am willing to make everything good,
that I just have to have time.

Merchant

It is something we would understand as wealth.
People do things for me,
and for those who do things for me,
and so on.
There is a base tolerance for my existence.
There is also a jealousy.
Most of the others have left or been killed.
I have gotten richer.
The estate has become the idol.
It is built up, out, weaker, and more frivolously, every day.
It has become a whole thing.
I only retain the right of hospitality.

Program

Join the clubs,
engage in campus activity,
learn,
practice, and be creative in the industry.

Safe Distance

I have crept up on them.
They are using stories to sell you something,
sad stories, the ones that need a hero.
They are aware that is considered abrupt and rude for them
to bring this up prematurely. It has to be done at the right time.
The repulsed throw the switch too early.
So do I.

Vulnerable

I venture in,

into the high grass now,
could be ripped apart at any moment.
Dusted and freshly cleaned house—
and a telephone conversation to minimize the time.
Talk to me!
My perfect life has to deal with this!
Give it to me real!
I hate talking with this thing!

Liars

People were wrong from the very beginning.
They say they witness things
that are either totally made up
or completely misinterpreted.

Ticker

Second time around and I am aware.
This is happening, this is happening, this is happening…
That instead of stuff happening.

Sin

Does there have to be a *doing something wrong*
to have a pleasurable experience?
Only if you want it repeated.
Only if you want to make someone new.

Direct Deposit

The people who don't have a job right now
will look at me who does have one

and say don't give up one paycheck.
Volunteer only so much of the other stuff,
none of that.

Defeated

What word has been resurrected lately? Collaborator?
I don't see it as good and evil.
I am currently underpaid and underutilized.
And I don't like the subliminal corporate culture either.
But I am here in my own workspace,
left alone for the most part,
doing the job well—
I will take that trade-off.

Beeps and Computer Sounds

The distortion turned into a wave
and slowed down to a rhythm.
It just took a little bit of both.
And then a series of them, looped.
Concentrate on that and not Kirk.
How long will it last?
Listen to it.
It lasts forever.
And now music over it. I can still hear it.
I can still hear the beat, the three in the series.

Life at the Pad

Some doctors are better than others.
The speaker out among the frogs,
belching out with them,

they don't seem to mind,
but I hear it.
One synthesized English speaking voice.
They should mind!
Why don't they?

Ashes

An obsessive thought fills the void, this person
must be changed. Yep, another one.
The irritant is not connected with fear, not this time,
sometimes it is just repulsion, then there's love,
the rest is just nothing, just irritation, like here.
It has a little higher brain function; a schedule
can be developed around it, a treatment plan.

Temple

But this is a holy land. You have stumbled upon it.
You've wandered in and now you're completely surrounded.
Some babble and babble and wander back on out.
We observe them and note down what they say.
Some just describe the exterior features,
estimate the dimensions,
just sit there.
They want to leave every second they're there.
We time gas station visits.

Gaps

This full frontal assault relies on terror and a quick surrender.
An ordered second line defense turns the massacre around,
one wave after another sometimes.

Novelty

Get away from them!
They overwhelm your senses.
Their art surrounds. It wants you to give way.
They want you to absorb.
Things to watch out for, if there is some kind of illicit
nature to it, and if there is someone constantly talking!

Bots

I have to have a scouting report.
Anonymity makes it harder.
I will be several different people.
I will question you with each.

Lunatics

The neural glia has a specialized function, a new one.
I am the same, people!
The neurotransmitters seem to jump where they're
supposed to go. This improves response time greatly.
What are you doing? Don't add more fluid!
The chipset's delay will be canceled out.
That is the plan anyway.

Bad

It's not because I am poor,
small, or different.
I am not.
I just wasn't taught much about anything.

Night Out

I look good with the buttons unbuttoned
and pale skin.
I like wearing the cheap watch. I like the way it looks.
I like my beard now. Not fully in.
I like the way my hair hangs with it.
I look wild.
It will grow longer and look bad.
It will get trimmed and it will look bad too.

1992

Sunshine that made a noise,
me tripping on headphones,
sometimes walking around,
plugging in,
charging for the first time.
Electrolytes—sometimes the song would last forever,
time would stop.

Virginia

I am quite shut in here.
But tell me! Victor is an artist?
He used to draw such funny things!
But it's still marvelous! Victor is an artist!
Does he have wonderful friends?
Is he happy?

Here Is a Case

Even though consciously it's about not getting the money,
everything else in the mind is that someone else is.

We are animals.
The more we can get rid of the animal part the better.
But it will always be.
Leaving other people alone, not knowing what they have,
that's me.

Cake

I get a techno, art deco, sophisticated
blast in the face every time.
It is hilarious as I think of it, but as it is happening,
an acutely made awareness of unworthiness
absolutely infuses my body,
especially under the influence.
It is a fake reality,
but it exists and it is triggered every single time.
This thing is alongside an extremely strong hominid ego.
I don't go to stores, I don't shop.

Shopping Day

It can't be too fancy, trendy.
I want to get nice things.
A store that's dumbed down, so to speak,
more mainstream,
has reached out in good faith.

Sheol

The artist's work is rejected.
Look at the bottom line, there is a loss.
Maybe in isolation, maybe a social success there.
Activities sent out digitally aren't respond to either.

Even with the same help, still a loss.
Your work and yourself are both rejected.

Three-Card Monte

It is an unfair game.
Rigged is not the right word.
Entered into falsely
and playing against someone highly skilled,
that is not fair.
The object is to win money, so the advantage is pressed,
a seeking out for one-on-one, skins, pool.

Rat Race

This is *Survivor Island*.
I don't want to stumble upon Richard.
The rules—trees, streams, storms, and ocean sometimes.
The dumbest rules ever.
Or so I thought.
Cameras outdo them all.

Suicide Cults

The fact that everyone's not convinced,
everyone's not converted,
that has to be part of it.
So few, and they had to be trained so hard.
There was supposed to be a fraction of humanity,
this isn't a fraction of anything.
Same boring thing, day after day.
And people have the same annoying habits,
these never seem to end.

Get supplies, check on the status of business,
eat, and be alone—no one is going anywhere.
Someone is sick or dying,
someone in holy matrimony,
someone new moving into the big house,
these add a Wednesday element to Tuesday.
When the terminal condition is mentioned
or the cops are on their way,
that's when things get serious.

All Crete Looked On

Some pilgrim named Icarus tried to leave,
tried to escape the tyranny.
He gathered up all his followers and told them he was God.
They all got into ships and drowned.

Black and White

The good guys and the bad guys always spoke their minds.
The townsfolk probably accepted things.
The good guys mostly were lawmen.
The outlaws stole something—
that's how the bloodshed usually began.

Labor

Why? Why would someone do that?
A modern civilized person? It's like
volunteering to be a doormat.
Hardly anyone's going to do that.
Pilgrims try to walk across deserts.

Sad Factory

Neuroses produce physical manifestations.
Twitching is one form of this,
larger body movements and actions too.
It is complex because it needs repression.
Twitching is when this wins.
Repression isn't overcome with courage
or a lack of conscience.
It isn't overcome.
It is still there stronger than ever.

Provisional

After a few years, the army will bring in people
that will straighten things out,
run things as they should be run.
Early retirements and staff redeployments
to lower level jobs are what will follow.

Modern Marauding Knights

There has to have been a golden age; anything's
better than this.
Not even a flag with a boar.
Just some loyalty
to some dark kingdom
that isn't understandable to anyone.
These people take their well-trained minds,
bring their weapons and strategies,
and just simply take everything in sight.

www.ingramcontent.com/pod-product-compliance
Lightning Source LLC
Chambersburg PA
CBHW031116080526
44587CB00011B/998